Fixing Issues with S3 Event Notifications

Table of Contents

Chapter 1. Introduction

Handling data in a digital realm can be an intricate and strategic endeavor. This Special Report is an essential resource for those who routinely maneuver through the nuances of AWS S3 event notifications and their associated challenges. Delving into this highly technical subject, we will take a comprehensive look at identifying and rectifying issues related to S3 Event Notifications. The content is meticulously designed to simplify complex concepts, ensuring even a novice AWS user can find value and apply the provided solutions effectively within their operations. The goal remains consistent throughout - to empower readers to streamline and fortify their processes, reducing the risk of data loss and enhancing overall operational efficiency. Therefore, whether you're an IT specialist looking to refine your skill set, or a burgeoning professional keen to tackle the intricacies of AWS S3, this report serves as a functional, valuable guide through the labyrinth of S3 event notifications.

Chapter 2. Understanding AWS S3 Event Notifications

Understanding AWS S3 event notifications can be distilled into several key areas, beginning with an elementary introduction of AWS S3 and its event notification feature. We then proceed to the setup process, followed by an illuminating discussion on common problems and their solutions, as well as best practices to consider.

First and foremost, let's lay a fundamental groundwork of what AWS S3 is. Amazon Simple Storage Service (S3) is a scalable object storage service offered by Amazon Web Services (AWS). Companies can store and retrieve any amount of data from anywhere on the web using S3, making it a convenient solution for backup and restore, data archiving, application development, and much more.

2.1. Event Notifications in AWS S3

One of the key features provided by AWS S3 is event notifications. This feature enables real-time, automated responses to changes in your S3 objects. Notifications are sent in response to specific events - such as a new object being created (via PUT request), an object being deleted, or a Reduced Redundancy Storage (RRS) object being lost. Depending on the configuration, S3 will deliver these event notifications as a message to an Amazon Simple Queue Service (SQS) queue, as an email through Amazon Simple Notification Service (SNS), or invoke an AWS Lambda function.

2.2. Setting Up Event Notifications

To set up event notifications in AWS S3, follow these five essential steps:

1. Identify the bucket for which you want to generate event notifications.

2. In the Properties pane, under the 'Event notifications' tab, click 'Create event notification'.

3. Define the event type(s) for which you want to generate notifications.

4. Choose a destination for the notifications (SNS, SQS, or Lambda).

5. Save the configuration.

It is essential to note that Amazon S3 won't publish an event unless you have permissions to set up notifications.

2.3. Understanding Common Problems

Even with the best setup, you may encounter some challenges when dealing with S3 event notifications. Some issues that you may encounter include:

1. **Missing or Delayed Notifications:** S3 notifications are usually delivered in seconds, but network issues or system load can cause delays. If you suspect missing notifications, consider using CloudWatch to monitor the system better.

2. **Unwanted Redelivery:** Occasionally, you may receive duplicate notifications. This is usually due to the 200 message acknowledgement that the system might not have received, thereby triggering a redelivery.

3. **Invalid Event Structure:** S3 notifications should match a specific JSON structure. Any alteration to this might cause parsing errors downstream.

In each of these cases, proper logging and appropriate exception handling are crucial for identifying and remedying the problems.

2.4. Solutions and Best Practices

Many solutions can be applied proactively to circumvent potential problems. Below, we've handpicked some valuable solutions and best practices when working with S3 event notifications:

1. Use deduplication logic within the consuming service to handle any duplicate notifications.

2. Employ a Dead Letter Queue (DLQ) to handle any problematic messages that continually fail.

3. Integrate with AWS CloudWatch to monitor your system. You can set up alarms to alert you for failed notifications.

4. Ensure that the event data structure is well-validated before processing, to avoid any parsing errors.

5. Use JSON schema validation to warrant the robustness of the message structure.

In conclusion, AWS S3 event notifications are a powerful tool, providing real-time, automated scalability. By understanding the setup process, common problems, solutions and best practices, you can effectively leverage this tool to build efficient and reliable systems.

Chapter 3. The Importance of Event Notifications in S3

To comprehensively understand the importance of Event Notifications in AWS S3, we need to delineate the core constituents of this subject, including AWS S3's functionalities, what Event Notifications entail and the relevance they hold within these mechanisms.

The Amazon Simple Storage Service (S3) is an object storage service that offers scalability, data availability, security, and performance. As a storage solution, it is used to back up and restore data, archive data, and host websites. Importantly, it also buttresses applications running on servers, building robust, scalable, and high-speed applications.

Event Notifications within AWS S3 are an integral component of the aforementioned uses. They allow automatic responses to various events, such as the creation (put) and deletion (delete) of objects. This real-time capability yields a wealth of benefits for your data management, facilitating system efficiency, user accessibility, and data integrity. Let's analyze these benefits in greater detail.

3.1. The Role of Real-time Monitoring and Response

Arguably the most significant aspect of S3 Event Notifications is real-time monitoring and response. AWS S3 Event Notifications typically help users and systems recognize and respond to changes within S3 buckets. They facilitate real-time alerts for modifications in an object's status, allowing you to promptly address changes and potential issues.

These notifications can trigger AWS Lambda functions, Amazon SQS queues, or Amazon SNS topics, thus enabling a swift, automated reaction to any modification, whether it be a new object creation or the deletion of an existing object. The importance of this real-time response cannot be overstated – it encourages system efficiency, aids in avoiding data loss, and helps maintain the overall health of an AWS application.

3.2. Simplifying the Audit Process

With the growth of industry requirements and regulatory standards, organizations are required to maintain a clear record and audit trail. AWS S3 Event Notifications provide log details for every change in the S3 bucket, making the audit process more straightforward and less time-consuming.

Additionally, AWS S3 notifications work seamlessly with AWS CloudTrail, automatically retaining logs and highlighting data changes that initiate compliance checking and enable post-event forensic investigations. This integration simplifies data governance and ensures a seamless trail for the audit process.

3.3. Streamlining Workflows

When AWS S3 Event Notifications get triggered, they can automate various workflow operations related to the object. This automation can include triggering Lambda functions to process data after an upload, replicating data to other areas, or executing housekeeping tasks like data transformation and cleanup.

The automation of such tasks reduces manual intervention and errors, and scales up the efficiency of the organization. By triggering the appropriate response, Event Notifications serve as a guardian against potential system hiccups, ensuring smooth operations.

3.4. Ensuring Data Integrity

The importance of maintaining data integrity within an S3 bucket cannot be sidelined. AWS S3 Event Notifications play a crucial role in this aspect, as they allow you to create a system of checks and balances by keeping track of deletions and modifications.

For instance, if an object is accidentally deleted by an end-user or malicious script, event notifications enable immediate alerting and automated restoration of the object, ensuring data longevity and system-deemed integrity.

3.5. Dovetailing with Other AWS Services

AWS S3 Event Notifications dovetail well with AWS ecosystems and services. For example, they work seamlessly with AWS Lambda to automatically run code without provisioning or managing servers, leading to task automation and enhanced operations. Furthermore, they can use the Amazon SNS topic to give messages across to multiple subscribers, or populate an Amazon SQS queue to decouple and scale microservices, distributed systems, and serverless applications.

In sum, AWS S3 Event Notifications bring a high degree of versatility, dynamism, and efficiency to your data management operations, from increasing response time to potential issues and facilitating auditing to streamlining workflows and maintaining data integrity. The importance of Event Notifications in AWS S3 is therefore inherently tied to the smooth operation of the services, and the ability to maximize the potential of AWS for the effective and precision-oriented running of applications and systems.

Chapter 4. Common Issues with S3 Event Notifications

Amazon Web Services' Simple Storage Service (S3) is a highly flexible storage facility that enables easy, quick, and secure data saving over the internet. S3 enhances users' workflow by incorporating event notifications triggered by specific events. Nevertheless, unlike every technical enterprise, ephemeral issues may occur, leading to operational inefficiencies. This section will progressively dissect common S3 Event Notification problems and offer strategic solutions.

4.1. Detecting Missed S3 Event Notifications

A recurring issue that many AWS S3 users encounter is missed S3 event notifications. This can often occur due to configuration errors and cause operational disruptions if not promptly identified and rectified.

First, it is crucial to ascertain the event sources that are correctly triggering notifications. As AWS S3 enables myriad event configurations, you should verify whether a specific event is configured to release notifications. In some instances, users inadvertently overlook certain events, leading to apparent notification absences.

For instance, if the 's3:ObjectCreated:*' or 's3:ObjectRemoved:*' are not included in the event types while setting up the S3 bucket, specific events such as creating or deleting a file in the S3 bucket might silently occur. The absence of these specifications implies that S3 event notifications remain untriggered when such events occur.

The missing S3 Event Notifications issue may also arise due to incorrect bucket policy. Ensure the configured IAM policies and S3 bucket policies permit S3 to invoke your Lambda function or send a message to your SNS topic or SQS queue.

The policies should be meticulously programmed to grant the 's3:PutBucketNotification' permission to allow updates to the notification configuration.

To examine if discrepancies exist within the event configuration, use the Amazon S3 console to navigate to the Notifications tab of the bucket. Above all, ensure the targeted event's name aligns with the event types highlighted by AWS to eliminate any instances of missed event notifications.

4.2. Inaccurate S3 Event Notification Delivery

Another frequent issue is the wrong delivery of S3 Event Notifications. Oftentimes, this issue arises due to improper setup of the endpoint for receiving notifications, such as Lambda, SQS, or SNS. You should verify if the endpoint is correctly set and has suitable permissions to receive notifications.

In the instance of using AWS Lambda as the endpoint, ensure the function is correctly set, particularly the execution role permissions. The execution role should have permissions to access the Amazon S3 bucket where your input files are stored, write logs to CloudWatch Logs, and if the function uses other AWS resources, include permissions for those resources.

Event delivery issues might also result from an inappropriately set-up SNS Topic Subscription. For example, if the HTTP/S endpoint is used as a subscriber to the SNS topic, ensure the endpoint is correctly subscribed and has been authenticated. Use the Amazon SNS Console to review the SNS Topic Subscriptions and confirm the delivery policy settings.

4.3. Handling Duplicate S3 Event Notifications

An equally important issue is the reception of duplicate notifications. Amazon S3 notifications are designed to provide at least once delivery. However, network blips or temporary unavailability of the destination service might cause S3 to retry the delivery, thus resulting in duplicate notifications.

The best approach to tackle this issue is to design idempotent receivers i.e., receivers that produce the same result even after processing the same message more than once. For instance, if you are using Lambda as your event receiver, your function should be written in such a way that it produces the same outcome for multiple invocations with the same event data.

Duplicate notifications can also be managed by using a 'deduplication queue'. The core function of these queues involves storing every received message. Upon receipt of a new message, the queue checks if the message was previously processed. If so, the queue discards the message; Otherwise, the message is processed and stored for future tracking.

In conclusion, navigating the labyrinth of AWS S3 event notifications and their potential issues is an essential skill for maximizing your data operations. By acquainting yourself with common problems and their solutions, you can build robust and reliable workflows that effectively leverage the power of AWS S3 and improve your overall operational efficiency. Regular audits of your AWS S3 event configurations, as well as continual learning and adaption of best practices, can reduce the chances of running into these familiar issues.

Chapter 5. Diagnosis of Event Notification Failures

Event notifications in AWS S3 are crucial elements for automating your workflows and responses. However, diagnosing event notifications failures can often present myriad difficulties due to their multifaceted nature. Individuals often struggle to pinpoint where the problem resides, thus stunting their progression. This segment will shine a light on these intricate details, providing a systematic understanding and approach towards diagnosing event notification failures in AWS S3.

5.1. The Concept and Importance of Event Notification Failures

A grasp of the fundamental concept holds paramount importance before any diagnostic endeavor can commence. AWS S3 Event Notifications are automated messages sent by S3 upon specific occurrences such as Put, Get, or Delete operations on an object. When functional, these notifications effortlessly trigger workflows to ensure seamless operations. However, when these event notifications fail, your entire workflow may hinder, potentially cascading into a larger issue affecting your operational efficiency.

5.2. Recognizing Symptoms of Event Notifications Failure

To recognize a failure in the S3 Event Notification system, you need to consider several key symptoms.

1. Unusual delays in workflow processes: If there are processes which should be automatically triggered but have an unusual

delay, this might be a sign of event notification failure.

2. Unexpected Workload Stoppage: Sudden and inexplicable stoppage of a workload can be another symptom. If the process that depends on the S3 Event Notification does not get started or gets abruptly halted, this could signify a problem.

3. Anomalies in Log Files: Log entries might not be generated for certain actions, or there could be error log entries related to notifications.

These symptoms often serve as the first indicators of potential issues within your event notification operations.

5.3. Setting Up Diagnostic Logs

Showcasing now is an essential tool for diagnosing event notification failures - AWS CloudWatch Logs. To detect and understand the issues, we advise setting up Diagnostic Logs:

1. Navigate to the AWS Management Console, and open the CloudWatch service.

2. Choose 'Logs' from the navigation pane and hit the 'Actions' button.

3. In the drop-down menu, select 'Create log group', entering a name for the new group.

4. Save your changes.

Through these logs, you can easily catch numerous errors and issues that could be affecting your S3 Event Notifications.

5.4. Common Problem Encounters and Solutions

Next, we explore common problem encounters revolving around S3 Event Notifications and potential solutions.

Missing Notification Configurations

You encounter this issue when the notification configuration that was originally set has been removed. To troubleshoot, review the configuration of your S3 bucket. If it seems void, refresh the notification configuration.

Lambda Function Errors

Lambda function errors are often associated with event notifications. The symptoms are typically an absence of your Lambda function invocation. To diagnose, verify that your Lambda function is functioning appropriately. Check your Lambda function log in CloudWatch, and correct any error that gets flagged.

Incorrect Bucket Policy or IAM Roles

The presence of an incorrect bucket policy or IAM roles can impede S3 event notifications from flowing freely. If so, consider validating your permissions. IAM roles should be granted with the proper access to publish notifications to the destined service. A flawed Bucket Policy could deny access, so ensure this is rectified to permit full access.

5.5. Use of Amazon SNS for Debugging

Another effective method for diagnosing AWS S3 event notification failures is leveraging Amazon Simple Notification Service (SNS). By creating an SNS Topic and coupling it with the bucket sending notifications, any event occurring in the bucket would trigger a message to be published to the SNS Topic. Here again, CloudWatch can be utilized to view logs of the incoming messages. This acts as a buffer from where you can identify if the notification was triggered from S3 and sent to the assigned target. Troubles arising beyond this are typically issues on the receiving end, instead of the S3 bucket itself.

Through a robust understanding of the symptoms and diagnostic practices, the diagnosis of event notification failures becomes that bit more manageable. This, in tandem with approaching the solution systematically, ensures an efficient resolution to the issues at hand. Above all though, nurture a habit of regularly reviewing your event notification setup – preventive observations may help you avert crisis before they manifest. Further chapters in this report will delve into more complex situations and nuances of implementing the optimal AWS S3 configuration.

Chapter 6. Methods to Debug and Solve Notification Errors

Implementing and maintaining AWS S3 event notifications isn't always a smooth sail, especially when errors creep in, causing potential disruptions in your system. Resolving these issues requires a deep understanding of not only the problem but also the diagnostic mechanisms and resultant solutions for efficient rectification. Let's embark on an in-depth journey into the various methods that can be utilized to debug and solve notification errors.

6.1. Debugging Event Notification Configuration

To ensure that the event notification system functions optimally, we must first ensure that the configuration settings are free from errors. An incorrect configuration might trigger notifications that fail to reach the intended destinations or cause inaccurate notifications.

In order to debug the configuration, access your bucket settings on the AWS S3 console. Check thoroughly to make sure:

- Correct events are selected.

- The event destination is configured correctly.

- That the S3 bucket policy allows S3 to invoke your function_for lambda functions, or SNS topic/ SQS queue can receive messages.

- That there are no mismatched configurations like different event destinations for the same types of events or poorly defined object keynames.

If you still face issues, identify whether there is a problem in the underlying AWS Lambda, Amazon SQS, or Amazon SNS by verifying their configuration settings.

6.2. Diagnosing Notification Issues with Amazon CloudWatch Logs

Amazon CloudWatch Logs provide a valuable resource for diagnosing notification issues. AWS automatically integrates this service, and you can use it to monitor your resources and applications, collect and store logs from your environment, and find and troubleshoot issues.

In the case of AWS Lambda functions, log streams are automatically created for the function, and these logs are invaluable in debugging issues. Similarly, for SNS and SQS, you can publish the delivery status of notification messages to CloudWatch log groups.

Use the CloudWatch console or AWS CLI to view the logs and identify any problems that may have arisen during the operation. CloudWatch Logs insights can also be used to further analyze the log data for patterns and outliers, helping you identify root causes.

6.3. Monitoring the Lambda Function

AWS Lambda functions play a vast role in S3 event notifications, and thus, monitoring Lambda becomes pivotal for debugging.

AWS services like CloudWatch and X-Ray give extensive insights into the Lambda function. While CloudWatch provides logs and metrics, X-Ray produces service maps to give you an overview of how your application is performing.

From information about request rates to error rates and what caused the errors along with other crucial details, these services can help you identify any faults in your Lambda function, thereby assisting in resolving any Lambda function-involved notification errors.

6.4. Confirming the Configuration of SNS/SQS

When setting up S3 event notifications, we sometimes direct the events to an SNS topic or an SQS queue. But what if notifications fail to reach these destinations?

In such cases, you must confirm the correct setup of SNS topics and SQS queues. Do ensure:

- The right access policy is in place.

- The necessary permissions are granted.

- Any dead-letter queues, if used, are correctly set up.

- The notification handler of the receiving end has been properly programmed to handle the incoming messages.

Cross-check this with the response metadata logged in CloudWatch Logs to ensure delivery.

6.5. Checking Lambda Function Execution Roles

A frequent cause of failure in AWS S3 event notifications is the misconfiguration of the execution role provided to the Lambda function.

Ensure that:

- The Lambda function's execution role has necessary permissions for the S3 and any other services it will interact with.

- It includes policies for `AWSLambdaExecute`, `AWSLambdaBasicExecutionRole`, and `AmazonS3ReadOnlyAccess` as a basic permission set.

By adhering to these guidelines, you assure that your AWS Lambda function has what it needs to interact with the specified AWS resources without security access issues.

6.6. Troubleshooting Delivery Failures

Sometimes, despite successful invocation of the Lambda function, SNS topic, or SQS queue, you may face delivery failures. To diagnose such issues, check the AWS CloudWatch Log Stream for the invoked service for any errors shown in the execution results.

For SNS or SQS, validate the receiving process at the endpoint to handle the incoming notifications correctly. For AWS Lambda, review coding errors or exceptions that might prevent the execution of your function.

This comprehensive detailing of the intricate methods to debug and solve notification errors will help you streamline your troubleshooting process. Always remember, diagnosing and rectifying errors is equally as crucial as developing systems. After all, even the sturdiest ship needs a seasoned seafarer at the helm to steer it safely through the storm.

Chapter 7. Case Studies: Real-life Troubleshooting of S3 Event Notifications

In this detailed exploration, we scope out real-life troubleshooting scenarios centered around S3 Event Notifications. Focusing on four specific cases, we outline the underlying issues, cross-examine potential remedies, and finally, highlight the most effective solutions.

7.1. Case 1: S3 Event Notification Not Triggering

One of the most common obstacles experienced with S3 Event Notifications is that they do not trigger as expected. This happens due to several possible reasons, including issues with your AWS Lambda function, problems with permissions, or configuration mistakes.

A user reported that after setting up an S3 bucket with an event notification to trigger a Lambda function, no event was triggered when a new object was uploaded to the corresponding bucket. This was found to be a two-fold problem:

1. The AWS Lambda function had incorrect execution role permissions.

2. The S3 bucket and AWS Lambda function were not situated in the same region, leading to the event notification failing subtly.

An investigation focused on discerning and solving this issue involved the following steps:

1. Ensured the AWS Lambda function had the correct execution role permissions by reviewing its IAM role. It was found initially to

lack the 's3:GetObject' and 's3:PutObject' permissions, which are crucial to read and write objects.

2. Realigned the S3 bucket and AWS Lambda into the same region, allowing them to interact without hindrance.

7.2. Case 2: S3 Event Notification Delays

Event notification delays can disrupt workflow continuity, making timely troubleshooting crucial. An enterprise reported significant lag within its S3 Event Notifications leading to operational disarray. The underlying problem reported was the delay in triggering Lambda functions connected to the S3 bucket.

To troubleshoot this problem, the potential reasons for these delays were considered:

1. Network issues between the S3 bucket and Lambda.

2. Invoking an already 'in-use' Lambda function.

To negate these issues, these steps were carried out:

1. Ran diagnostic speed tests repeatedly between the S3 and Lambda, making sure the network path was without obstructions.

2. Provisioned adequate concurrency reserves for the Lambda function, ensuring it would be available each time an operation needed to be triggered in the S3 bucket.

7.3. Case 3: Duplicate S3 Event Notifications

While working with S3 Event Notifications, you might occasionally encounter duplicate notifications. A user reported such an instance where the same event notification was triggered several times for a single object upload.

Potential reasons for this scenario include:

1. Policy misconfiguration, leading to event redundancy.

2. Existence of multiple notification configurations for the same event type on the bucket.

Here's how this complex issue was addressed:

1. Audited and corrected bucket policies and notification configurations, removing any overlaps and redundancies.

2. Made sure that there was just one notification configuration for each event type, which resolved the problem of duplicity.

7.4. Case 4: S3 Event Notification Fails in EventBridge

Using Amazon EventBridge to manage S3 event notifications provides added flexibility, but it could concoct its own set of challenges. A user experienced failures while trying to route S3 event notifications through EventBridge.

The main contributors to such a problem could be misconfiguration of event rules or issues with target assignments and permissions.

Addressing this problem entailed the following steps:

1. Ensured EventBridge rules correctly matched the event pattern required for S3 event notifications.

2. Reviewed and amended target assignments, confirmed that EventBridge had necessary permissions to invoke the designated targets.

These real-world cases provide valuable insight into some potential stumbling blocks in the operation of S3 event notifications, adding direction to troubleshooting routines. Remember, every setback is unique, and earning quick victories over tribulations requires an understanding of the AWS ecosystem and a methodical problem-solving approach. By dissecting these cases, we hope to arm you with the knowledge to combat and fix S3 event-related issues more effectively.

Chapter 8. Best Practices for Maintaining S3 Event Notification Health

The health of your S3 Event Notification system is paramount to ensuring operational efficiency. From data transfer to storage, the functionality of Amazon S3 hinges on effective communication between different AWS services. In light of this, we delve into an exhaustive list of best practices aimed at keeping your S3 Event Notifications running optimally.

8.1. Monitoring and Alerting System

You should leverage AWS CloudWatch and S3 event logging for reliable monitoring and alerting. Monitoring your event notifications is the first step toward maintaining their health. AWS CloudWatch offers comprehensive monitoring solutions, including automated system checks and timely alerts. You can set up CloudWatch alarms to notify you when a certain threshold of failed event notifications is surpassed.

You can also use S3's built-in event logging feature. This logs all events so you can manually verify their success and better identify any occurring patterns of failure.

8.2. Identifying Failed Deliveries

Failed deliveries can be the result of many reasons. One common issue is permissions. Your S3 bucket and the receiving service must have the correct IAM roles and permissions. Even minor configuration changes can cause event delivery to fail. Be sure to regularly cross-check your permission settings.

Failed deliveries can also occur due to a non-responding, overworked, or incapacitated endpoint. Keeping an eye on the receiving endpoint's health and swiftly addressing any issues drastically reduces the chances of failed event notifications.

8.3. Handling Duplicate Notifications

While S3 strives to eliminate duplicates, under certain circumstances it may deliver the same event notification multiple times. Therefore, the target of the S3 Event Notification should be developed with idempotency in mind. That is, repeated processing of the same event notification should not trigger unforeseen side effects, guaranteeing the system's overall robustness.

8.4. Retry Policies

Implementing a robust and efficient retry policy helps to overcome the intermittent failures likely to occur in a distributed environment. AWS provides automatic retries and backoffs for S3 Event Notifications for services like AWS Lambda, SQS, and SNS. However, it's crucial to understand the default and maximum retry policies for the respective services and configure them according to the system's needs.

8.5. Controlling the Rate of Notifications

In cases where your system is overwhelmed with the quantity of notifications, AWS allows you to configure a throttling policy. This is particularly beneficial when dealing with large-scale data processes or when your endpoints have specific service limits that you don't want to exceed.

Uploading objects in large batches can trigger a surge of event notifications, potentially straining your system. To avoid this, consider staggering object uploads or applying random prefixes to object keys to distribute the requests evenly and prevent hot partitions in Amazon S3.

8.6. Managing Dead-Letter Queues

Sometimes, an S3 Event Notification might fail even after multiple retries. To avoid the loss of such notifications, you can configure a dead-letter queue (DLQ) where they can be safely stored for a later examination. DLQs help maintain operational efficiency in the face of temporary setbacks, and reduce the chance of losing valuable information.

8.7. Checking the Status Code

Event notifications can fail for a variety of reasons. However, by just focusing on the most apparent causes, you risk failing to catch some of the less obvious ones. Therefore, it is critical to assess the status code returned by the system after each event notification request. This low-level checking can uncover any hidden abnormalities that might escape a cursory check of the system.

These best practices, coupled with a pragmatic and persistent approach, will certainly prove invaluable in maintaining the health of your AWS S3 Event Notifications. By aligning these practices with your operational strategies, you can ensure a stable, secure, and smooth functioning of your AWS S3, thus empowering your enterprise with enhanced capability and flexibility.

Chapter 9. Tools and Utilities for Monitoring S3 Event Notifications

To effectively administer and troubleshoot S3 event notifications, an assortment of tools and utilities are available. They can be broadly categorized into AWS-native services, third-party solutions, and do-it-yourself practices. We will evaluate these from numerous standpoints - usage, configuration, and practicality, aiming to provide insights into the most functional options suited for specific use cases.

9.1. AWS-native Services

Understanding AWS's built-in monitoring services is crucial to comprehensively managing and troubleshooting S3 event notifications.

Amazon CloudWatch: The pioneer among these is Amazon CloudWatch, a robust monitoring service that provides insightful data and actionable insights to holistically monitor the health of your AWS resources, applications, and services which run on AWS and on other platforms. It can be used to collect and track metrics, collect and monitor log files, set alarms, and automatically respond to changes in your AWS resources.

If you've enabled CloudWatch logs for your AWS Lambda function, metrics for the Lambda function's AWS/S3 event notification operations are automatically sent to CloudWatch. It gives real-time visibility into all Lambda function invocations, errors, and throttling.

Configuration involves:

- Enabling Amazon CloudWatch Logs in your Lambda function

configuration.

- Creating a new IAM role with enough permissions to write data to Amazon CloudWatch Logs.

Amazon Simple Notification Service (SNS): For real-time notifications of your S3 bucket events, Amazon SNS is an excellent service. When an event is detected in your S3 bucket, Amazon SNS can send you a message containing details of the event. These notifications can help you become aware of issues, such as changes to a bucket or unauthorized access as soon as they occur.

Configuration involves:

- Creating a new S3 bucket or selecting an existing one.

- Under Bucket properties, selecting Events.

- Adding a notification destination.

9.2. Third-Party Tools

While AWS-native services provide considerable monitoring capabilities, third-party tools can bring additional value with enhanced features and more user-friendly interfaces.

Datadog: Datadog is a monitoring service for cloud-scale applications. Its S3 integration comes with built-in dashboards and filters the bucket size, object counts, and more. Using AWS tags, you can filter and aggregate views for a more intricate perspective.

Configuration generally involves:

- Configuring the AWS integration.

- Inputting your S3 buckets in the Datadog AWS integration tile.

New Relic: New Relic is a performance management system that can monitor your entire AWS environment, including AWS S3. It provides a unified view of your environment, helping you understand how different services are connected and how their performance is affecting your applications and end-users.

Configuration involves:

- Setting up the New Relic AWS integration.

- Adding the AWS integration to your New Relic One dashboard.

9.3. Do-It-Yourself Processes

In addition to using tools and services, it's important to develop practices that allow you to proactively manage S3 event notifications and swiftly adapt to any changes. This approach provides resiliency, safety, and better preparation for anomalies affecting your S3 event notifications.

Auditing & Compliance Checking: Regularly auditing and checking your S3 bucket configuration, including S3 event notification settings, is a must. Track any changes made and ensure only necessary adjustments occur. This can be accomplished either manually or by using scripting utilities.

Alert Threshold Customization: Depending on your individual organizational needs, the default alert thresholds in your monitoring tools might not be fully applicable. Make sure to set and regularly update alert rules and thresholds which effectively flag irregularities without triggering false alerts.

Route Tracing: Tracing your S3 event notification route can help identify bottlenecks, points of failure, or inefficiencies. This involves manually following the path that an S3 event notification takes from the moment it's triggered to when it's processed.

By strategically employing a combination of the above-mentioned tools and practices, you can significantly improve your processes of monitoring and troubleshooting your S3 event notifications, helping you avoid data loss and elevate overall operational efficiency.

Chapter 10. Preventing Future Failures in S3 Event Notifications

To solidify the understanding of AWS S3 event notifications, it is imperative we delve into the preventive measures that could guard against future failures. It is crucial to ensure smooth operations and diminish the risk of data loss, which this section meticulously aims to address.

10.1. Understand Your Notification Configuration

Understanding your S3 event notifications configuration is the first step towards error prevention. As having only one or no notification configuration means that you don't get enough information when a process fails and not having any means that you are oblivious to activity in your buckets. This makes recovery extremely difficult and is a sure shot recipe for disaster. Always check that all your actions relevant to the triggered event are included in the configuration and that event notifications are enabled on all relevant S3 buckets.

10.2. Regular Auditing and Monitoring

Regular auditing and monitoring is another effective way to prevent future failure and inconsistencies. It allows you to isolate and promptly respond to any issues before they snowball into serious problems.

Audit your event notifications using AWS CloudTrail logs, which offer a near real-time stream of API calls. Use this stream to recognize patterns, track down errors, and detect anomalies. It is recommended to use AWS CloudTrail in combination with CloudWatch alarms to get timely alerts whenever there is an error with the event notifications.

10.3. Consistent Error Handling

Error handling is at the heart of robust software systems. Resilient software is expected to function well in the face of both programmatic and system errors. Focusing on consistent error handling will help ensure lack of alignment or coding errors do not lead to future failures.

S3 event notifications use Lambda functions as event handlers. You can try to impose some error handlers on Lambda functions and verify if error retries are conveniently set.

If the Lambda service encounters an error while executing the function, or if a function times out, it will be executed again by default. So, for the cases that are not idempotent, we have to be careful on how we set our error retries.

10.4. Implement Dead Letter Queues (DLQ)

When dealing with AWS Lambda and synchronous invocations (which are common with S3 event notifications), it's essential to design a good system for handling errors. One way is to implement a Dead Letter Queue (or DLQ). DLQs collect and store unsuccessful messages for later analysis, ensuring that no vital data is lost in the wilderness.

In Lambda, you can set up a DLQ to hold failed events for functions that cannot be processed. By using DLQ, you can analyze unsuccessful executions and diagnose any issues that prevented a function from being processed.

10.5. Enforce Robust Security Measures

Security is indisputably crucial to all AWS operations. Ensuring that your buckets and functions are secure can save you from potential data breaches or loss.

Use AWS Identity and Access Management (IAM) policies to control who can send and receive S3 event notifications. Explicitly deny permissions if there's no need for a user or group to access notifications.

Moreover, encrypt your data at rest and activate default encryption on all your S3 buckets. This way, anyone uploading an unencrypted object will get it automatically encrypted.

10.6. Testing and Simulating Failures

Finally, regular testing and failure simulations can help identify potential issues before they become real problems. Simulate failure scenarios to ensure your system can handle and recover from catastrophic events.

Use AWS Fault Injection Simulator (FIS) to set up and run controlled experiments. FIS injects faults and monitors responses in order to make your applications more resilient.

In conclusion, preventing future failures in S3 event notifications revolves around meticulous understanding, auditing, and proactive error handling. Armed with these strategies and the knowledge to execute, you are more equipped to shield your AWS operations from debilitating data loss and maximize operational efficiency.

Chapter 11. Continual Improvement Strategies for AWS S3 Operations

In the vast domain of Amazon Web Services (AWS), continual improvement is paramount for maintaining operational efficiency with S3 services. The operative optimization strategies and techniques play an essential role in preventing data loss and ensuring high productivity.

11.1. Understanding S3 and Its Capabilities

AWS S3 (Simple Storage Service) is an object storage service that offers industry-leading scalability, data availability, security, and performance. It allows you to store and protect any amount of data for a range of use cases, such as websites, mobile applications, backup and restore, archive, enterprise applications, IoT devices, and big data analytics.

However, with a wide range of possibilities comes a myriad of hurdles that need to be rectified to exploit the platform's full potential. Here are some pointers for understanding the comprehensive workings of S3 and the various areas you can target for continuous improvement.

11.2. Performing Periodic Audits

One of the key steps to continually improving AWS S3 operations is conducting regular audits. This encompasses checking access permissions, making sure logging is enabled, and pinpointing any non-compliant configurations. AWS's native service, AWS Config, comes in handy to audit and monitor the S3 bucket configurations and identify non-compliant resources.

Apart from AWS Config, you can leverage S3 Server Access Logging and AWS CloudTrail for auditing. However, be mindful that while Server Access Logging provides detailed records for the requests made to your bucket, CloudTrail logs API calls for your S3 bucket.

11.3. Monitoring and Notifications

AWS's native CloudWatch service allows monitoring your AWS resources and the applications that you run on AWS. CloudWatch alarm is a particularly convenient feature for setting high and low thresholds for metrics. When a threshold is breached, AWS can send a message to an SNS topic, which could then be emailed to admins, or trigger another AWS service via a Lambda function.

Furthermore, S3 Event Notifications can be configured to automatically notify when certain events happen in the connected S3 buckets. Notifications can be through either Amazon SNS, SQS, or AWS Lambda, thereby keeping you informed about the processes and alerting you in real-time to take swift actions when needed.

11.4. Establishing Data Lifecycle Policies

An effective data lifecycle policy is instrumental in reducing storage costs and ensuring the right data is in the right place at the right time. To automate the lifecycle management of data within your S3 buckets, AWS provides a feature called S3 Lifecycle Policies. This could help move older data to cheaper storage classes or automatically delete data that is no longer needed after a certain period.

For example, 30 days after an object's creation, it could be moved to Standard-IA (infrequent access), and after 60 days, an object might be moved to Glacier, a storage class designed for data archiving.

11.5. Implementing Backups and Versioning

To ensure data resilience and durability, it's always wise to have S3 bucket data backup somewhere. There are several strategies to backup S3 objects, like manual backups or cross-region replication.

S3 also offers a versioning capability, which can be used as a means of backup. When you enable versioning for a bucket, S3 automatically archives all versions (including all writes and deletes) of an object into the bucket. Hence, it's easier to retrieve previous versions of an object or recover one that's accidentally deleted.

11.6. Access Control and Security Measures

Access Management is a critical aspect of S3 operations. It's crucial to understand and effectively manage who has access to your S3 resources and know what activities they perform.

IAM (Identity and Access Management) controls in AWS provide granular access control for AWS services. Consider consolidating your access permissions in IAM policies to exert fine-grained control over your S3 operations. Additionally, employ S3 Bucket Policies and Access Control Lists (ACLs) to manage access to individual buckets.

Moreover, AWS provides advanced features such as encryption for additional security. All objects can be stored in S3 in an encrypted form. Amazon provides multiple methods for encryption, such as Amazon S3 managed keys, AWS Key Management Service, and

Customer-Provided Keys.

To inflate operational efficiency and sustain continual improvement within your AWS S3 service, it is crucial that you follow a well-defined, disciplined approach, keeping in mind all the aspects discussed above. By so doing, you'll not only leverage AWS S3's full capabilities but also enhance your operations, achieve cost-efficiency, and avoid potential pitfalls associated with data loss.